AMERICA'S MILITARY

By John Hamilton

VISIT US AT
WWW.ABDOPUB.COM

Published by ABDO & Daughters, an imprint of ABDO Publishing Company, 4940 Viking Drive, Suite 622, Edina, Minnesota 55435.

Printed in the United States.

Edited by: Tamara L. Britton and Kate A. Conley
Graphic Design: Arturo Leyva, David Bullen
Cover Design: Castaneda Dunham, Inc.
Photos: AP/Wide World, Corbis, Department of Defense

Library of Congress Cataloging-in-Publication Data

Hamilton, John, 1959-
    America's military / John Hamilton.
     p. cm.--(War in Iraq)
    Includes bibliographical references and index.
    Summary: Presents information on the twenty-first century Army, Marine Corps, Navy, and Air Force of the United States, including their history, role, structure, and equipment and supplies.
    ISBN 1-59197-492-5
    1. United States--Armed Forces--Weapons systems--Juvenile literature. 2. Military weapons--United States--History--21st century--Juvenile literature. 3. Iraq war, 2003--Equipment and supplies--Juvenile literature. [1. United States--Armed Forces. 2. Military weapons--United States.] I. Title. II. Series.

UF503 .H355 2003
355.8'0973'0905--dc21
                                 2003051931

TABLE OF CONTENTS

America's Military 5

The U.S. Army 8

The U.S. Marine Corps 16

The U.S. Navy 22

The U.S. Air Force 28

Special Operations Troops .36

Web Sites 43

Timeline 44

Fast Facts 46

Glossary 47

Index 48

Technology such as the stealth bomber makes the U.S. military the most advanced in the world.

AMERICA'S MILITARY

The United States Department of Defense is responsible for creating and maintaining military power. It uses this capability to protect America and advance its interests in the world. Today, the United States has the most powerful military on the planet. It is the only nation able to use effective large-scale military operations far beyond its borders, with little or no help from other countries.

U.S. forces do more than protect America from direct threats. They also maintain peace and stability in regions critical to U.S. interests. The United States also uses its military to bring peace to regions torn by ethnic or religious conflict. And it helps people suffering from natural disasters, such as hurricanes or earthquakes.

The United States has many advantages in maintaining its military might. The country has more than 200 years of military tradition to learn from. Compared with much of the rest of the world, the United States is wealthy and can afford to spend vast sums on its military. America's armed forces are equipped with the most advanced and lethal weapons systems available. High-tech weapons, such as precision-guided smart bombs, give the United States a major advantage over other countries on the battlefield.

As of September 2000, the country's armed forces had more than 2.65 million active-duty and reserve soldiers. It also employed nearly 700,000 civilians. In 2002, the Department of Defense budget was $312 billion. The United States spends more on defense than several of its allies combined, plus Russia and China. Advanced weapons are tremendously expensive. It costs $6.6 billion to build only three new Virginia-class attack submarines.

Big defense budgets and advanced weapons alone do not make a great military. General Omar Bradley once said, "Battles are won by the infantry, the armor, the artillery, and air teams, by soldiers living in the rain and huddling in the snow. But wars are won by the great strength of a Nation—the soldier and the civilian working together."

This drawing shows the new Virginia-class attack submarine. It is a stealth nuclear-powered submarine used in both deep- and shallow-water missions.

THE U.S. ARMY

The Unites States Army began on June 14, 1775. The Continental Congress created a national armed force to defend colonial cities from British forces. From the beginning, the young country depended on citizen soldiers. These were regular people who gave their time—and sometimes their lives—to defend their country. This contrasted sharply with how other countries formed their armies. They often relied on paid professionals and even freelancers from other countries. Great Britain, for example, hired many Hessian mercenaries from Prussia to fight during the American Revolution.

U.S. Army Insignia

The Continental Congress chose General George Washington as the army's first commander. Together with French allies, Washington led the army to victory over the British at the Battle of Yorktown in 1781. Once free from British rule, the United States kept the army intact to "provide for the common Defense" of the young nation.

At first, the army was used simply to defend U.S. territory from invaders. Later, especially during the past century, the army has been called upon to defend America's interests in other countries. Since its beginning, the army has fought in more than 175 military campaigns. It has soldiers stationed in more than 100 countries worldwide.

The backbone of the army is the infantry, foot soldiers who fight on the ground and occupy enemy territory. Occupying territory and keeping it from the enemy is the infantry's main job. During Operation Iraqi Freedom, several army units traveled to the Middle East to destroy the regime of Iraq's dictator, Saddam Hussein. Air power destroyed many enemy forces and weakened their key defenses, but the war wasn't won until ground forces occupied and controlled Iraqi territory. Approximately 255,000 American troops were deployed in the region during the war.

This Abrams battle tank is loaded on a cargo plane that will be deployed to Iraq.

Although individual soldiers on the ground are relatively weak and unprotected, the United States backs them up with advanced weapons and communications. The United States has one of the world's most effective ground forces thanks to tools such as antitank rocket launchers, Global Positioning System (GPS) receivers, and protective clothing.

The U.S. Army is heavily mechanized, which means it uses a variety of vehicles to gain speed and firepower advantage over the enemy. Tanks are a fearsome part of the army's mechanized force. Not only do heavy battle tanks protect infantry, they also destroy enemy tanks and armored vehicles. Today's army uses the M1A1 Abrams main battle tank for most of its combat armor duties.

Even before ground troops and armored vehicles engage the enemy, the army uses artillery to attack from far away. Artillery, big guns that hurl explosives at the enemy, can cause massive damage without exposing ground troops to enemy fire. Much of today's artillery is self-propelled, with huge guns on tracked vehicles that look like tanks.

An extremely important part of today's army is air cavalry. Helicopters can strike the enemy, transport troops, and evacuate the wounded. For attacking enemy troops and vehicles, the army often relies on AH-64 Apache helicopters. These machines fly across the battlefield at more than 100 miles per hour (161 km/h). They destroy tanks from a distance of almost 20,000 feet (6,096 m) using Hellfire missiles. Apaches are also fearsome weapons against enemy soldiers. They can fly in all weather, and at night, which is the preferred time for the army to fight enemy forces.

The Third Infantry Division is a highly mobile army unit that strikes hard and fast using armored vehicles and air support. The Third Infantry is nicknamed Rock of the Marne for its battlefield accomplishments during World War I. During Operation Iraqi Freedom, the unit was based first in Kuwait, and then pushed into southern Iraq, west of the city of Basra.

The Third Infantry is a mechanized infantry organization. It contains approximately 18,000 troops. They are supported by AH-64 Apache attack helicopters and artillery. The Third Infantry played a key role in fighting Iraq's Republican Guard forces.

At dawn on March 20, 2003, the first day of the invasion of Iraq, the Third Infantry charged forward with more than 1,000 vehicles. It advanced to the Euphrates River Valley in

The army's Third Infantry Division uses armored
vehicles for quick, powerful advances on Iraqi targets.

less than six hours, showcasing its role as a rapid strike force. From there the division turned northwest, heading toward the Iraqi capital. In just over two weeks, the Third Infantry Division swept across hundreds of miles of desert, battled Iraqi resistance, and then rolled into the western edge of Baghdad. Initiative, speed, and stealth were elements essential to winning in Operation Iraqi Freedom.

The U.S. Army's 101st Airborne Division is an air-assault unit. It uses the firepower of 281 helicopters, including Apache attack helicopters, to strike deep in enemy territory. Known as the Screaming Eagles, the unit claims that it is the only air assault division in the world. With 16,000 troops, the 101st Airborne helped protect the Third Infantry Division as both units headed north toward the Iraqi capital. In Operation Iraqi Freedom, the 101st Airborne successfully parachuted into several Iraqi airfields and secured them for coalition forces to use as forward bases. The 101st Airborne also destroyed Republican Guard units protecting Baghdad and other Iraqi cities.

The army's Eighty-second Airborne Division is smaller than the 101st Airborne, with approximately 5,000 troops. The Eighty-second Airborne is a quick-reaction force. It most often attacks at night, seizing targets such as airfields, usually

by parachute or helicopter. It secures the targets until reinforcements arrive. The Eighty-second Airborne can also rush into target areas within hours of getting the order.

GENERAL STRUCTURE OF U.S. ARMY FORCES

Squad/Section: 9–10 soldiers

Platoon: 16–44 soldiers

Company/Battery/Troop: 62–190 soldiers

Battalion/Squadron: 300–1,000 soldiers

Brigade/Regiment/Group: 3,000–5,000 soldiers

Division: 10,000–15,000 soldiers

Corps: 20,000–45,000 soldiers

Numbered Army: 50,000+ soldiers

THE U.S. MARINE CORPS

The United States Marine Corps began on November 10, 1775. The Continental Congress ordered the creation of the marines because American warships needed skilled, well-armed troops aboard. In those days, ships often rammed into each other during battle and grappled together. Men then fought hand-to-hand combat for control of the ships.

Today, the Marine Corps has much more independence, so much so that some people are surprised to learn it is still part of the Department of the Navy. The Marine Corps still

U.S. Marine Corps Insignia

provides security aboard U.S. warships, but its main job is to

seize beaches and naval bases so that larger U.S. forces can start land warfare against the enemy. The Marine Corps is so highly trained and well equipped that it is also used as an independent force in land campaigns, a role it played during Operation Iraqi Freedom.

Leathernecks, as marines are often called, are highly skilled and trained. They practice commando-style warfare, striking the enemy with quick and hard-hitting surprise attacks. In many ways, the marines are an entire department of special operations troops, though they are not technically classified this way. Still, they're often the first to go into harm's way when difficult assignments must be carried out.

Marines use a variety of special equipment to carry out their missions. These include amphibious assault vehicles, attack helicopters, and Harrier jump jets, which can land and take off vertically. Their ability to use airborne assault vehicles is one reason marines can attack the enemy far inland, not just on the beaches. Though they continually prepare for such attacks, the marines have not launched a large-scale amphibious beach assault since 1950. Instead, marines are most often used in small-scale conflicts around the globe, where rapid strikes are crucial for victory. One of the basic rules in warfare is "get there first with the most."

The fast-striking marines are highly capable of carrying out that order.

In Operation Iraqi Freedom, the Marine Corps fought with elements of the First Marine Expeditionary Force (MEF). The First MEF comprises several marine units, including the First Marine Division, support personnel, and several air wings. For security reasons, the United States did not say exactly how many marines were in Iraq, or where they were attacking during the drive to capture Baghdad.

The First Marines, which are based in Camp Pendleton in California, are famous for winning the Battle of Guadalcanal in World War II. In the war with Iraq, thousands of marines attacked from the south in Kuwait, crossed the Euphrates River, and then pushed northwest toward Baghdad. The first soldier to die in Operation Iraqi Freedom was from the First Marines. He was killed trying to secure an oil station in southern Iraq.

Within three weeks, the marines had helped dominate the enemy and had captured Baghdad. They used more than 100 F-18 and AV-8B planes and AH-1 Cobra attack helicopters to first attack the enemy. On the ground, the marines used a potent force of artillery, tanks, light armor, and infantry.

Marines used F-18 fighter jets, such as this one, during the initial air assault on Iraqi targets.

The commander of the First Marines was Lieutenant General James T. Conway, who also served in the Persian Gulf War. Emphasizing the Marine Corps's strength of striking hard and fast, he told his troops, "This isn't a fair fight. We didn't intend it to be."

U.S. Marines positioned near An Nasiriya, Iraq, during Operation Iraqi Freedom

U.S. lieutenant general James T. Conway (center)

THE U.S. NAVY

The United States Navy began on October 13, 1775, when the Continental Congress authorized two ships to be outfitted with guns and ammunition. With that authorization, the Continental navy was born. Many ships were soon added to fight during the American Revolution.

At first, the navy was mainly used to protect America's shores from invasion. Starting in the 1890s, the navy was used to prevent national security threats before they reached the United States.

Today, the navy is used to project American power worldwide. Water covers 70 percent of the earth's surface.

U.S. Navy Insignia

A missile launched from a U.S. battleship shoots past two other navy ships.

Most of the planet's population lives within 200 miles (322 km) of a shoreline. This makes it difficult for an enemy of America to be unaffected by U.S. naval forces.

Modern surface warfare uses task forces, or battle groups, which are groups of about a dozen ships. Each group usually consists of one big ship, such as an aircraft carrier, accompanied by smaller support vessels such as destroyers, frigates, and cruisers. Task forces are almost always accompanied by at least one attack submarine, mainly for protection from enemy subs. The ships travel and work together, combining the best of their antiair, antisurface, and antisubmarine strengths. Many supply ships loaded with fuel, food, and equipment escort task forces when they go to sea.

During World War II, it became clear that large battleships were no match for waves of torpedo-launching airplanes. Although today sea-launched cruise missiles are increasingly important to the navy's war strategy, aircraft carriers are still the most important ships in the fleet. Planes can be used to determine where the enemy is hiding. They also project power hundreds of miles inland. The United States has the largest and best-equipped aircraft carriers in the world. The USS *Theodore Roosevelt*, for example, can transport up to 85 aircraft and nearly 6,000 people.

Navy ships power toward the Middle East in battle groups of up to 12 vessels.

During Operation Iraqi Freedom, several carrier task forces were deployed to the Persian Gulf, the Mediterranean Sea, and surrounding areas. The carriers included the USS *Nimitz*, USS *Theodore Roosevelt*, USS *Harry S. Truman*, USS *Constellation*, and USS *Kitty Hawk*. During the war, the navy deployed approximately 60,000 maritime servicemen and servicewomen in the region, including the five carrier battle groups. Carrier-based warplanes repeatedly struck targets deep within Iraq, destroying air-defense equipment, command bunkers, and concentrations of enemy troops. More than 7,000 sorties, or missions, were flown, including surveillance and intelligence-gathering missions in support of ground troops.

The U.S. Navy is unchallenged in undersea warfare today, especially since the collapse of the Soviet Union in 1991. Its fleet of nuclear-powered submarines can stay under water for weeks or months at a time. Advanced electronics and sensors keep the submarine's crew informed of enemy ships and subs from far away. The U.S. submarine fleet can strike the enemy with accurate, long-range torpedoes, cruise missiles, and ballistic nuclear missiles.

Navy submarines are a feared force that can project U.S. power anywhere in the world. At one time, military experts believed submarines would eclipse aircraft carriers and other surface ships as the most important vessels in the navy's fleet. Recently, however, cruise missiles have been effectively deployed and launched from surface ships, increasing their range of striking power. Still, submarines are a crucial part of the U.S. military's total network of weapons.

The U.S. Navy uses nuclear submarines to launch torpedoes, cruise missiles, and nuclear missiles at enemy targets.

THE U.S. AIR FORCE

Modern aviation began on December 17, 1903, when Orville and Wilbur Wright made their famous 12-second flight at Kitty Hawk, North Carolina. In World War I, airplanes were first used successfully to find out where enemy forces were on the battlefield. Later, they were used to fight forces both on the surface and in the air.

During World War II, all sides used airplanes in increasing numbers. Air squadrons at that time were mainly under the command of the U.S. Army. After the intense air combat of World War II, the Army Air Service was granted independence and became the United States Air Force.

U.S. Air Force Insignia

A B-2 Spirit, B-1B bomber, and B-52 bomber fly together over Iraq. Air force pilots ran hundreds of bombing missions during Operation Iraqi Freedom.

One of the most important jobs of a nation's air force is reconnaissance, figuring out where enemy forces are hiding or moving around on the battlefield. Supporting troops on the ground, or acting as close air support, is another important mission. The U.S. Air Force gathers information, which gives U.S. forces a huge advantage on the battlefield. To gather this information, the air force uses tools such as detailed maps, radar tracking, and GPS receivers.

Because of this detailed knowledge of the enemy, U.S. jets and bombers can strike hard and with great accuracy. Taking advantage of this treasure trove of intelligence are GPS- and laser-guided bombs and missiles, moving target displays, and many other advanced electronics. U.S. Army, Navy, and Marine aviators also use these advances. In the best-case scenario, by the time ground troops arrive, enemy forces are reduced to scattered groups of soldiers that can barely resist.

During Operation Iraqi Freedom, air force strikes cut off enemy forces from their commanders. Many troops were shell-shocked by high-flying aircraft that they could barely see, let alone shoot back at. When waves of U.S. ground troops arrived, many dispirited Iraqi troops threw down their weapons, tore off their uniforms, and fled the battlefield.

The air force had done its job of taking the fight out of the enemy, which reduced U.S. casualties.

Recent developments in air force reconnaissance technology are drones such as the RQ-1 Predator. Drones are remotely operated robot planes. First used effectively in the war in Afghanistan, Predator drones presented a formidable challenge to enemy forces in Operation Iraqi Freedom.

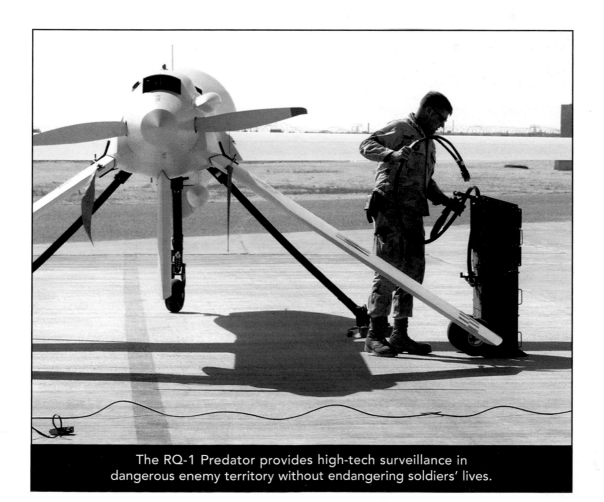

The RQ-1 Predator provides high-tech surveillance in dangerous enemy territory without endangering soldiers' lives.

Predators have a skin of bullet-resistant Kevlar, and they can remain aloft on marathon missions of 20 hours or more. They have powerful cameras that give ground operators a real-time view of the battlefield, and they can spot the enemy more than 20 miles (32 km) away. In addition to their reconnaissance abilities, Predators can also be armed with Hellfire antitank missiles mounted under each wing.

The air force has another powerful reconnaissance system at its disposal. Joint Surveillance and Target Attack Radar System (JSTARS) is a special radar built into the Boeing 707 aircraft. The air force developed this system with the army. It is used to track group troops and vehicles. Air commanders can now track a complete battle in real time. JSTARS data is passed on to ground commanders and fighter airplanes, which allows for quick and accurate strikes.

Fighters and bombers are the backbone of the U.S. Air Force arsenal. U.S. pilots constantly practice air-to-air combat techniques. By destroying the enemy's planes, the United States makes the enemy blind and gains uninterrupted reconnaissance ability. Air-to-air combat has evolved from World War I, when pilots shot at each other with pistols and rifles. Today, sophisticated tracking electronics allow pilots to fire missiles at the enemy from several miles away.

The JSTARS radar on the bottom of this Boeing 707 allows military commanders to view ground targets and troop movements in real time.

Approximately 80 percent of air victories occur because a defender is shot down before he has detected the attacker. Making the initial contact is a huge advantage in aerial warfare. By using advanced reconnaissance electronics, U.S. pilots have a crucial edge in finding the enemy and shooting first.

When an aircraft is called up to shoot a particular enemy target, it is called a strike mission. Pilots call these air-to-mud missions. There are many dangers to overcome when flying fast and low, including antiaircraft fire, other planes, and even the ground itself.

The air force now relies on stealth aircraft to hide from the enemy, especially during the early stages of war. Aircraft like the B-2 bomber and F-117A Nighthawk fighter use special radar-evading designs, paint, and jamming electronics to hide from the enemy. This allows the planes to sneak deep into enemy territory and destroy air defense weapons so other U.S. aircraft can safely enter enemy airspace.

An important development in recent years is the use of smart missiles and bombs that use GPS- and laser-guided systems to find their targets. Precision-guided bombs were used in the majority of air-to-ground missions during Operation Iraqi Freedom. They are more effective in

destroying enemy targets, and they also reduce the chance of civilians being killed accidentally. Civilian casualties were a big concern in Iraq because the forces of Saddam Hussein often hid their weapons and troops close to human shields.

The EA-6B Prowler provides cover for two
F-14 bombers by jamming enemy radar systems.

SPECIAL OPERATIONS TROOPS

Besides their regular fighting forces, the U.S. Army, Navy, and Air Force train and equip elite groups of special operations troops, sometimes called special ops. The U.S. Marine Corps also includes special operations units, but they are tightly woven into their regular forces.

Special operations soldiers are highly intelligent, as well as specially educated and equipped. They are very good at sneaking into enemy territory and striking hard and fast. They call themselves the quiet professionals, and often get the most challenging assignments in wartime. These elite troops have become more and more important on today's battlefield, where victory depends more on stealth and surprise than simple brute force.

Special operations troops are often called on to use their advanced training and weapons on politically sensitive missions. On missions like these, failure could harm the United States, so only the best-trained soldiers and most advanced weapons are used.

Special operations troops are elite soldiers from all branches of the U.S. military. They are specially trained to carry out the most dangerous missions.

Operation Iraqi Freedom saw the largest use of special operations forces since the Vietnam War. Many covert, or secret, troops were operating inside Iraq several months before the war started. Some worked closely with agents from the Central Intelligence Agency, which relies on its own group of special operations soldiers.

Most special ops troops during the war in Iraq were American. Some also came from the United Kingdom and Australia, and several other coalition countries. Most special operations missions occurred in northern Iraq, where troops worked with Kurdish fighters against Saddam Hussein's regime.

U.S. Army Rangers parachute into dangerous territory.

Special ops troops successfully called in air strikes against enemy armor and troops by "painting" them with laser light. The laser tags helped U.S. bombers pinpoint enemy positions with precision-guided bombs and missiles.

Special ops troops in Iraq also attacked targets such as airfields, sites where weapons of mass destruction may have been stored, and command and control headquarters. Special ops troops also assisted conventional forces in the south of the country as they fought their way toward Baghdad.

Each armed service trains and operates its own special operations groups. The Army Rangers are the U.S. Army's elite light-infantry troops. Training is extremely difficult. Candidates learn to parachute from airplanes, climb mountains in full battle gear, descend from helicopters on special ropes, and fight their way out of enemy territory with little food or sleep. Only the physically and mentally toughest are chosen to be Army Rangers. Two-thirds of candidates fail to complete ranger training on their first try.

Candidates selected to be rangers are sent on the most dangerous missions. They strike quickly to take over airfields or harbors ahead of regular troops. They are trained to operate in harsh terrain including jungles, mountains, and even snowy glaciers. Typical missions include guerrilla warfare, raids, ambushes, and secretly gathering information about the enemy.

The Green Berets are Army Rangers who are especially talented and intelligent. They often work with foreign groups, frequently in remote and hostile lands. The Green Berets help these groups fight against governments that are enemies of the United States. For example, the Green Berets aided the Kurdish forces fighting Saddam Hussein's regime in northern Iraq. The Green Berets are experts with weapons, as well as unarmed combat. They are also extremely smart. Most are experts at foreign languages and cultures, and they use their knowledge to train local forces.

Green Berets troops are also sent on clandestine missions deep inside enemy territory. Groups of 12 Green Berets are called A-Teams. One of their most important duties is to "paint" enemy forces from a distance with laser beams so that U.S. airplanes can use precision-guided bombs and missiles. A-Teams can operate for weeks inside enemy territory without help from regular troops. In addition to helping out U.S. airplanes, they are also trained to gather information and to ambush the enemy.

The U.S. Navy has a special operations unit similar to the Green Berets called Navy SEALs. The term *SEAL* stands for Sea, Air, and Land. SEALs trace their history to the skilled sailors of World War II. They operate in 16-member teams and are especially skilled at underwater missions. They are also trained to attack targets on land and to gather information for regular ground forces. SEALs can fight in the desert, jungle, or city.

The U.S. Army has a third special forces unit called the Delta Force. It is so secret the Pentagon doesn't officially admit that it exists. It is recognized as the most elite of all special forces, and draws its members from all the different armed services. Everything about the unit, including its makeup and strength, is a closely guarded secret. It is equipped with the most advanced technology and weapons the United States can provide. Hostage rescue is one of the unit's specialties.

The U.S. Air Force has its own elite unit, called the Air Force Special Operations Command. This group is specially trained for search-and-rescue. They also provide close air support for ground troops, and they resupply special operations units.

A Navy SEAL lowers himself from a helicopter.

Sometimes special forces units are not even human. For example, the U.S. Navy uses a team of 65 bottle-nosed dolphins, 15 sea lions, and 2 whales to help detect mines that might harm U.S. ships. These highly trained animals are also used to haul tools to underwater laboratories, and even to locate combat divers. The navy calls them Marine Mammal Systems, and they are part of Navy Special Clearance Team One, which specializes in clearing underwater mines.

Dolphins are especially reliable and trainable sea animals. They use an internal system of clicks and snaps to send sound waves through the water. When the sound waves strike an underwater object, the returning echo is picked up by the dolphin's mandibular nerve, which allows the dolphin to sense the object.

Underwater mines are usually tethered to an anchor. Dolphins are trained to locate mines and then attach a buoy marker to their tethers so that underwater teams can later deactivate or destroy the mines. Special waterproof cameras can also be attached to a dolphin's dorsal fin so that trainers can monitor what is happening under water. Operation Iraqi Freedom is the first time dolphins have been used to detect underwater mines in wartime. They were especially helpful in detecting mines in the port of Umm Qasr in southern Iraq. This was very important so that ships could safely bring in humanitarian relief supplies for Iraqi citizens.

WEB SITES
WWW.ABDOPUB.COM

To learn more about America's military, visit ABDO Publishing Company on the World Wide Web at **www.abdopub.com**. Web sites about America's military are featured on our Book Links page. These links are routinely monitored and updated to provide the most current information available.

The U.S. Navy used specially trained dolphins to detect mines in the Persian Gulf while it worked to secure ports for incoming supply ships.

TIMELINE

1775

June 14: U.S. Army created by Continental Congress
October 13: U.S. Navy created by Continental Congress
November 10: U.S. Marine Corps created by Continental Congres

1781

U.S. Army defeated British forces at the Battle of Yorktown

1890s

U.S. Navy first used to prevent national security threats before the
reached the United States

1903

December 17: Orville and Wilbur Wright made first airplane fligh
in Kitty Hawk, North Carolina

1947

September 18: U.S. Air Force became independent from Army
Air Service

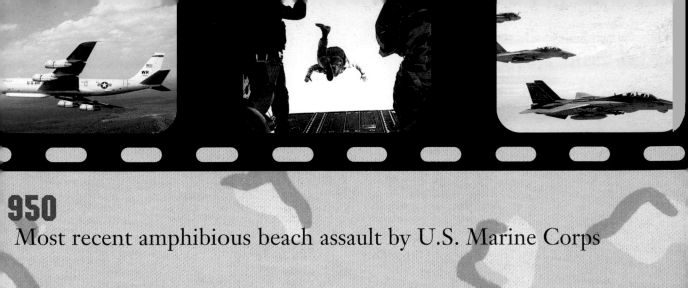

950

Most recent amphibious beach assault by U.S. Marine Corps

991

Persian Gulf War
Collapse of the Soviet Union

2002

U.S. Department of Defense budget is $312 billion

2003

March 20–May 1: U.S. and allied forces used military action to overturn the Iraqi government during Operation Iraqi Freedom

FAST FACTS

- The U.S. Army, Navy, and Marine Corps were established in 1775 by the Continental Congress.

- In 1903, Orville and Wilbur Wright flew the first airplane in Kitty Hawk, North Carolina. They were only able to stay in the air for 12 seconds.

- The U.S. Army's Third Infantry Division is sometimes called Rock of the Marne. It earned this name from its accomplishments during World War I.

- In September 2000, the United States had more than 2.65 million people enlisted in its military as active duty or reserve soldiers.

- The U.S. Army's 101st Airborne Division is also known as the Screaming Eagles. It has 281 helicopters, which it uses to attack enemies.

- The U.S. Marine Corps is part of the U.S. Navy. It conducts operations both at sea and on land.

- Marines are sometimes called leathernecks.

- The U.S. Navy has submarines that can stay under water for weeks or even months at a time.

- Several of the aircraft carriers that went to the Middle East during Operation Iraqi Freedom were the USS *Nimitz*, USS *Theodore Roosevelt*, USS *Harry S. Truman*, USS *Constellation*, and USS *Kitty Hawk*.

- The U.S. Navy uses dolphins, sea lions, and whales to help find underwater mines, to help locate human divers, and to bring tools to underwater laboratories. The navy used bottle-nosed dolphins for such purposes during Operation Iraqi Freedom.

- During Operation Iraqi Freedom, about 255,000 American troops were stationed in or near Iraq.

GLOSSARY

amphibious:
Operating on both land and water.

casualty:
A soldier or civilian who is injured or killed in an act of war.

civilian:
Someone who is not a member of the military.

clandestine:
Something that is secret.

Continental Congress:
A group of lawmakers in the colonies at the time of the American Revolution.

dictator:
A ruler who has complete control and usually governs in a cruel or unfair way.

human shield:
People who attempt to stop a military attack by using their bodies as shields.

maritime:
Relating to the sea.

Pentagon:
The huge, five-sided building near Washington, D.C., where the main offices of the Department of Defense are located.

real time:
The actual time during which something takes place.

smart bomb:
A bomb or missile that navigates its way to a target, often by following a laser beam "painted" on the target by a plane or special operations soldier on the ground. Smart bombs are very accurate.

stealth:
Having the ability to go undetected by radar.

INDEX

A
Afghanistan 31
AH-1 Cobra helicopter 18
AH-64 Apache helicopter 12, 14
Air Force Special Operations
  Command 41
American Revolution 8, 22
amphibious assault vehicle 17
Army Rangers 39, 40
Australia 38
AV-8B 18

B
Baghdad, Iraq 14, 18, 39
Basra, Iraq 12
Battle of Guadalcanal 18
Boeing 707 32
Bradley, Omar 6
B-2 Bomber 34

C
Camp Pendleton 18
Central Intelligence Agency 38
Conway, James T. 20

D
Delta Force 41

E
Eighty-second Airborne Division
  14, 15
Euphrates River 12, 18

F
F-117A Nighthawk 34
F-18 18
First Marine Division 18, 20
First Marine Expeditionary Force
  (MEF) 18, 20

G
Global Positioning System
  (GPS) 11, 30, 34
Green Berets 40

H
Harrier jump jets 17
Hellfire missiles 12, 32
Hussein, Saddam 9, 35, 38, 40

I
Iraq 9, 12, 18, 26, 35, 38–40, 42

J
Joint Surveillance and Target Attack
  Radar System (JSTARS) 32

K
Kurds 38, 40
Kuwait 12, 18

M
Marine Mammal Systems 42
Mediterranean Sea 26
M1A1 Abrams tank 11, 12
M2A2 Bradley fighting vehicle 12

N
Navy Special Clearance
  Team One 42

O
101st Airborne Division 14
Operation Iraqi Freedom 9, 12, 14,
  17, 18, 26, 30, 31, 34, 38, 42

P
Pentagon 41
Persian Gulf 26
Persian Gulf War 20

R
Republican Guard 12, 14
RQ-1 Predator 31, 32

S
SEALs 40
Soviet Union 26

T
Third Infantry Division 12, 14

U
Umm Qasr, Iraq 42
United Kingdom 38

V
Vietnam War 38
Virginia-class attack submarine 6

W
Washington, George 9
World War I 12, 28, 32
World War II 18, 24, 28, 40
Wright brothers 28